LESSON BANK

Reports, Articles and Advertisements

Mary Green

Contents

Belair Publications

Acknowledgements

First published in 2000 by Belair Publications.
United Kingdom: Belair Publications, Albert House, Apex Business Centre, Boscombe Road, Dunstable, LU5 4RL.

Editor: Gaynor Spry
Layout artist: James Brown
Cover design: Martin Cross
Illustrations: Noya Miller

Page 33: 'Work hard for Victory' and 'Hitler will send no warning' from Topham Picturepoint. 'Careless Talk Costs Lives' used with the permission of *The Trustees of the Imperial War Museum*, London.

Page 38: Bugmobile idea and illustration from *Penguin English Project Stage One – Things Working* edited by Penny Blackie (Penguin).

Page 45: Article from *The Guardian* Tuesday December 17, 1996.

Every effort has been made to contact copyright holders of material used in this book. If any have been overlooked, we will be pleased to make any necessary arrangements.

British Library Cataloguing in Publication Data. A catalogue record for this book is available from the British Library.

Mary Green hereby asserts her moral rights to be identified as the author of this work in accordance with the Copyright, Designs and Patents Act 1988.

ISBN 1 84191 081–3

Introduction

Children need to develop a range of skills to understand reports, articles and advertisements. At a simple level they need to be able to recognise the layout and features of newspapers and other media. They also need to know how to distinguish between fact and opinion, to consider different viewpoints and identify an audience. This book addresses these and other skills.

Reports, Articles and Advertisements has been written for children aged 7–11 years and has been divided into two sections: Part 1 covers skills and topics for 7–9 year olds, Part 2 covers skills and topics for 9–11 year olds. There are eleven chapters in all, with four pages to each chapter. These four pages comprise: one teacher page, one resource page and two activity sheets. The resource pages and activity sheets are photocopiable. The teacher page provides supporting notes, giving advice and information, and is organised as follows:

Background provides information on the chapter, particularly the content of the resource page and its function.

Learning Objectives outlines the skills on which each chapter focuses.

Introduction suggests points to be covered when talking to the class in the first part of the lesson. This section also offers advice on using the resource page as a learning focus with a group of children. Each resource page includes a Talking and Thinking section which you might like to refer to during group activities.

Using the Activity Sheets explains how to reinforce the learning introduced on the resource page through the activity sheets. In the early chapters, these activity sheets focus on tasks such as matching, sequencing and note taking. In the later chapters, more complex tasks are covered, such as looking at methods of persuasion and how to present an argument. Several subject areas, Geography and History in particular, are addressed as well as English.

Follow-up and Extension Ideas offers suggestions on developing the skills covered in each chapter. These may include teaching activities or independent activities for the children. This section also provides suggestions for research work or long-term tasks that may involve specific subject areas and the use of ICT.

Belair Lesson Banks on CD

All Belair *Lesson Banks* come in a CD format as well as book format. The CDs offer children the opportunity to work on a computer, a learning tool they often find stimulating, while working through the same high quality activities found in the book.

Key features

- The discs have many activities on them including responding to pictures, writing frames, working in tables, sorting and matching activities, and scored 'multi-choice' questions.
- Many of the activities can be altered. If you, as the teacher, want to modify the language or change a question, you can do so easily. You can make changes such as:
  - simplify the text
  - add complexity to the language and structure
  - provide model answers or examples.
- Each screen has a linked screen which gives the children an opportunity to write an extended piece in response to a question. The linked screen will automatically print out with the original screen.
- Finally, you can of course modify the activities on screen and print them out for the children to use as paper activities.

ideas page

Communicating Information

Background

The children are encouraged to recognise that reading matter comes in a variety of printed forms, usually has a limited and specific purpose and is often disposable. The resource page **What's In Print?** asks the children to identify three printed forms and discuss their features, while the activity sheets **What Am I For?** and **More Messages** focus on the functions of printed material. **More Messages** also asks the children to distinguish between print and electronic media.

Learning Objectives

- To recognise that printed information is presented in a variety of ways
- To understand that much printed information:
  - has a specific purpose
  - is disposable
  - can combine handwriting and typed text
- To distinguish between printed matter and electronic media
- To understand what a document is

Introduction

- The children should recognise easily the different kinds of printed information on the resource page, but need to focus on their forms and functions, distinguishing clearly between each example.
- Once the children have understood that printed material is varied, carry out a brainstorming activity. Record how many different kinds of printed material the children can think of and the purpose of each.
- Discuss how printed information is communicated to us (for example, adverts as leaflets, on hoardings, as posters; letters, printed and handwritten, by post). Reinforce this discussion with the activity sheet **What Am I For?**
- Ask the children if they would keep any of the examples on the resource page, and if so, which ones and why. Birthday cards may be kept for sentimental reasons, school reports are sometimes kept into adulthood (again for similar reasons) while magazines usually have a limited life. The children can suggest further examples that only have a brief life, such as flyers.

Using the Activity Sheets

What Am I For?
When completed the children could discuss other uses of the Yellow Pages and newspapers.

More Messages
This activity sheet follows on from the previous one and is the more difficult of the two. Other ways to find information include: CD-ROMs, The Internet, by radio, by word of mouth. The extension work introduces electronic media.

Follow-up and Extension Ideas

- Ask the children to observe what type of printed material comes through the letterbox at home, over a week, and suggest what should be kept and what should be thrown away. They could record the information in the form of a chart or construct a graph.
- Provide a range of printed material in the classroom that the children can study and classify. (Include examples of official documents explaining that they are often legal and as such are meant to be permanent. Note also that they are written in authoritative and archaic language.)
- You may wish to focus on particular printed forms, for example, newspapers – comparing tabloid and broadsheet, looking at layout such as ratio of photos to text.
- Discuss electronic media further: computers, television, radio, video, telephone. You could demonstrate how a fax machine works.
- Provide the children with opportunities to see how information is located on screen, by scrolling and using the mouse.
- If you wish, discuss how most printed media is now produced using electronic methods.

What's In Print?

Look at the pictures below.

Fleetwood Lane Primary School Report
Name: Warren Hill

SUBJECT	COMMENTS	LEVEL
English	Warren has worked very hard this year. I am pleased	3

Talking and Thinking

- What do the pictures show?
- Who would read each source and why?
- Which would you save? How long for?
- What is each one made of?
- Who has written each one?
- Which would you buy and where?
- Think of two ways in which a book is different from the items shown above.

What Am I For?

Match each sentence to the correct picture by drawing a line.

1. I tell you how much money you have to pay.

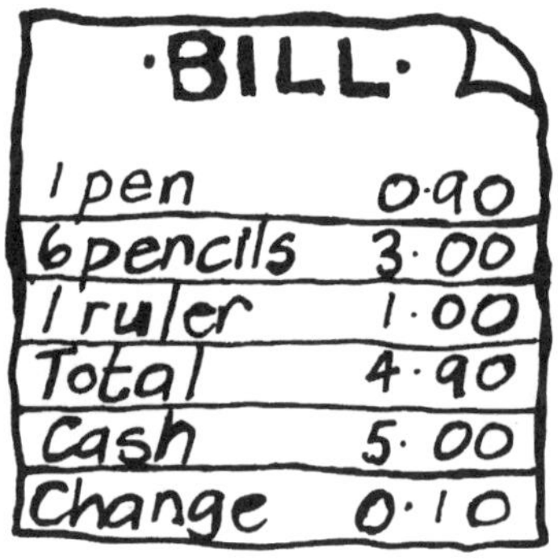

2. I tell you when you were born.

3. You can find a phone number in me.

4. I tell you which way to go.

5. I give you the news every day.

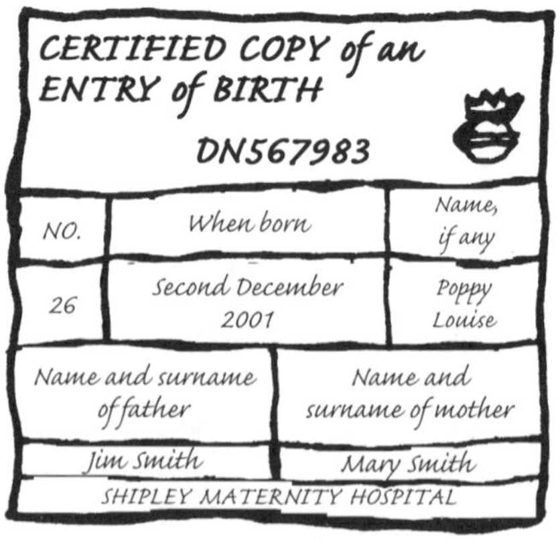

CERTIFIED COPY of an ENTRY of BIRTH

DN567983

NO.	When born	Name, if any
26	Second December 2001	Poppy Louise

Name and surname of father	Name and surname of mother
Jim Smith	Mary Smith

SHIPLEY MATERNITY HOSPITAL

6. I am selling something.

NOW

- Write down one more thing you can read.
- Explain what it is used for.

More Messages

1. Printed information is all around us. Think about why you would read the following.

calendar

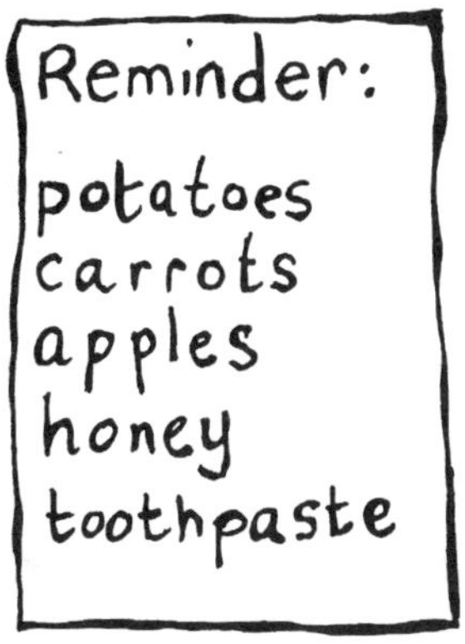

list

labels

poster

2. Look at the printed information in your classroom and write down seven different kinds. Say why you would read each one, like this:

Printed information	**Why I would read it**
Twenty Terrible Tongue Twisters	I would read these to make me laugh.

NOW Printed material is not the only way to find information. We can watch television, for example. Think of three more ways we can find information.

ideas page

Presenting the Same Event in Different Ways

Background

The resource page **Read All About It** shows the sinking of the Titanic presented in book form and through a newspaper. You may need to explain the events to the children. Many will have seen film versions and while the children may think they know what happened they are unlikely to distinguish between fact and fiction. The film provides a useful opportunity to do this. The first activity sheet, **The Titanic**, presents the series of events leading to the disaster. The second, **Presentation**, looks at further ways of presenting the events.

Learning Objectives

- To recognise that the same event or story can be presented in different ways
- To recognise different media including electronic media
- To describe events
- To distinguish between fact and fiction

Using the Activity Sheets

The Titanic

This activity relates to the discussion about fact and fiction under Introduction.

Presentation

Other forms to present what happened might be: cinema, computers, paintings and photos. The tasks involved on this sheet are a useful preparation for the study of sources at a later stage.

Introduction

- Ask the children to decide what the illustrations on the resource page are. (Both the book (non-fiction) and the newspaper purport to present the facts.) Ensure they understand the events involved and can separate facts from fiction. (See fact box below).
- Talking and Thinking provides opportunities to discuss the nature of the media involved and you might wish to reinforce earlier work done under Communicating Information (see page 4).
- You may then wish to turn to the activity sheet **The Titanic** before discussing further ways of presenting events.

Follow-up and Extension Ideas

- If possible, collect a range of material which presents the sinking of the Titanic in different ways for the children to examine. Encourage them to discuss not only different kinds of presentation, but also which are likely to be historically accurate.
- Collect a range of media concerned with the same events (historical events such as the Gunpowder Plot can be fruitful) and ask the children to compare the presentations.
- Ask them to examine the different ways in which they themselves present information; for example: a daily diary, story, drawings and writing. You could also look at diagrams and charts, such as weather charts, which can be viewed as documents.
- Once the children are familiar with the differences they can present their own experience or a familiar event in two distinct forms such as a story, a newspaper article or a diary. Writing frames constructed to support different language styles could be provided here.
- More able children could discuss the best way of presenting different kinds of information. They can work in groups to do this, using focus cards. For example, write the heading at the top of a card 'Which Would You Choose and Why?'. Underneath the heading write an example (such as a bus timetable, or a story with a safety warning) with suggestions for presenting this information (such as a diagram, cartoon, book, CD-ROM, poster). The children must choose the best way, coming to a consensus as a group. The more difficult cards would present them with choices that were not so clear-cut.

Titanic Fact Box

- It was on its maiden voyage from Southampton to New York.
- It struck an iceberg about 153km south of Newfoundland on April 14, 1912.
- There were over 2,220 persons aboard, about 1513 died.
- Lifeboat space had only been provided for half the passengers.
- The wreck was not found until July 1986.

Read All About It

Look at A and B.

A.

B.

Talking and Thinking

- What is A? What kind of information would it give?
- Where would you find it?
- What is B? Who would read it?
- Where would you buy it? When?
- In what way are both sources the same? Think of two reasons.

The Titanic

Look at the pictures and write a sentence under each one saying what happens. The first has been done for you.

The Titanic leaves Southampton on its first voyage.

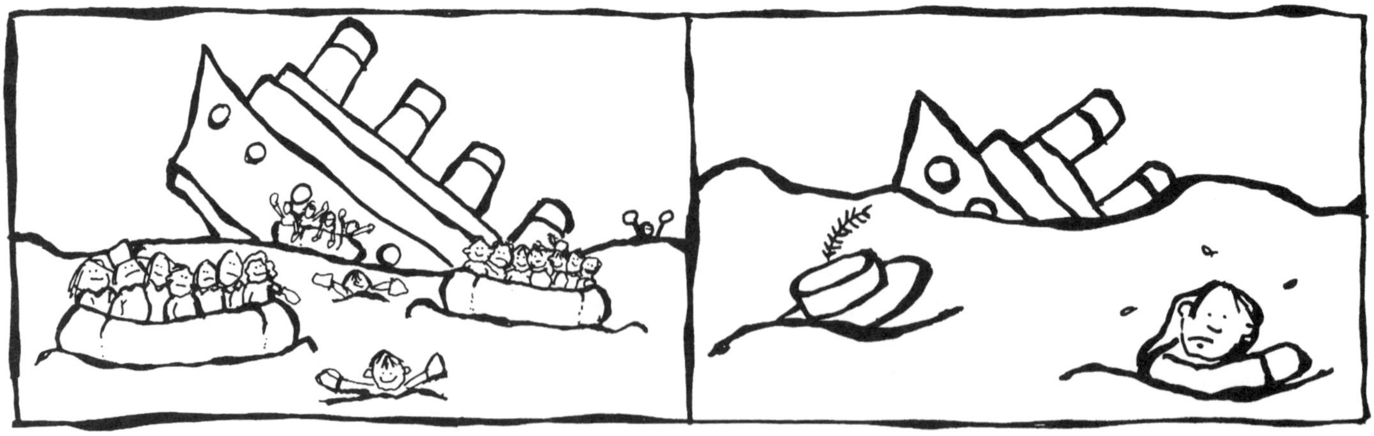

NOW Write down two facts about the sinking of the Titanic.

Presentation

In what other ways can we tell people today about a disaster?
Write the correct name under each picture.

comic	video	poster	telling someone
television	radio	letters	government reports

NOW Write down two other ways to present what happens in a disaster.

ideas page

Comics

Background

Although comics are primarily fiction they often include letters, instructions and puzzles. They can also be used to highlight some of the features of newspapers and magazines, introducing younger children to the idea of audience and advertising. The children should consider that comics are designed the way they are in order to sell. Free gifts, for example, highlight this (though more importantly the ultimate appeal of comics lies in their focus on children's concerns, such as avoiding or escaping trouble, opportunism and food). How far children identify with particular cartoon characters and their adventures can be the key to the comic's success. The resource page **The Pipsqueaks** is a front page layout of a typical comic for 7–9 year olds.

Learning Objectives

- To understand the layout and features of a front page
- To recognise that the front page:
  - gives information on contents
  - is an advertisement for the comic
- To understand that there is an intended audience

Introduction

- Ask the children what the picture is of, who they think **The Pipsqueaks** are and what kind of things they do. You may wish to draw comparisons with well-known cartoon characters in comics, for example, Dennis the Menace.
- Turn to the layout, asking the children what the comic contains and how they know. Look at the different layout features. Ask the children why particular words are prominent. Discuss the questions under Talking and Thinking, focusing on the purpose of the front page.
- Colour is an important feature of a comic and the children might like to colour in the cover on the resource page, making good use of bright and eye-catching colours. This page will also be a useful reference later on when the children design their own front page. The resource page is simpler in design than the front pages of most comics.

Using the Activity Sheets

The Front Page
This activity sheet is the easier of the two sheets and asks the children to identify particular features of the front page. It can act as preparation for the second sheet.

My Ideal Comic
Having completed the work involved in the resource page and **The Front Page**, the children should be ready to consider how they would create their own comic: what they would include in it, their intended audience and so on. They are encouraged to construct notes, and then use these notes to write about their ideal comic. Please note, the children are asked to write in short notes and later in sentences and you may wish to discuss the differences before the children begin.

Follow-up and Extension Ideas

- Collect a range of comics and ask the children to compare their front pages, noting common features and also important differences. They can also distinguish between fiction and non-fiction contents.
- Ask them to decide on the age range of the target audience for different comics.
- With help, the children can create their own comic, as an extended task. They can work in groups, making simple policy decisions regarding audience, cost and what to include. They can also divide tasks amongst themselves and use ICT for final drafts. Templates for picture crosswords and other puzzles should be provided and any appropriate work the children are following elsewhere, such as letter writing, can be included. Making a comic is useful preparatory work for creating class newspapers. (See the chapter Newspapers which starts on page 24.)
- The children can consider where else they would see cartoon characters (for example, television, film, video) and what their purpose is (for example, entertainment, advertising).

The Pipsqueaks

Talking and Thinking

- How is the front page of the comic laid out? Find: the title, contents, bullet points.
- What else can you find?
- Which words are written in capital letters? Why do you think this is?
- Why do you think so many comics have free gifts?
- Why do you think the front page is important? Think of more than one reason.
- What comics do you read? What else could you buy for the same price? Do you think comics are good value for money?

The Front Page

Read the questions and circle all the things in the columns that are true.

How much does the comic cost?	50p	90p	£1.10	25p
How often is the comic published?	daily	weekly	monthly	annually (every year)
Who would read the comic?	teachers	boys and girls	mothers	grandparents
What punctuation is used?	capital letters	full stops	commas	speech marks

Write down why you think most comics use exclamation marks and capital letters.

My Ideal Comic

Write notes as answers to the questions.

1. What age range is your comic for?

   ___

2. List all the things you would include in your ideal comic.

   ___

   ___

3. Give your comic a title. ___
4. How often will your comic be published? ___
5. How much will it cost? ___

Now use your notes to write five sentences about your ideal comic.

My Ideal Comic

___

___

___

___

___

___

ideas page

Fact and Opinion

Background

On the resource sheet **Cows on the Move** the children are asked to study a picture of four cows causing chaos at a busy crossroads. They should imagine that they are eyewitnesses. Help them to identify the facts shown in the picture, assess how people are responding and try to deduce the cause of the incident. The first activity sheet, **What Comes Next?**, presents information about the cause; the second, **Which is Which?**, deals with fact and opinion.

Learning Objectives

- To identify facts
- To recognise effects
- To deduce the cause
- To sequence events
- To distinguish between fact and opinion

Introduction

- Ask the children to study the picture and sum up what is happening.
- Turning to Talking and Thinking they should note the details: where the cows are; what they are doing; the problems created; what the people in the picture are doing. You may wish to record some of these points under 'facts'.
- The children could then consider how the people might feel about the incident and their opinions on what has happened.You could record these points under 'opinions'. (Point to the varied expressions on the characters' faces. The children could compare the faces of the irate drivers with the children laughing. They could also decide how the cows might feel!)
- You may also wish to discuss what has happened as 'effects' and how it has happened as 'causes'.

Using the Activity Sheets

What Comes Next?
The causes of the incident are presented here in the wrong order and the children must sequence them correctly. The correct order is: A herd..., Someone left..., Four cows..., They wandered..., They travelled..., They caused... . The information is presented as facts. No opinions are expressed.

Which is Which?
In this activity sheet opinions about the incident are expressed and the facts reiterated. The children must distinguish between the two to complete the chart. Work covered so far should help the children here. Answers: Facts: A, D, E, F, H. Opinions: B, C, G.

Follow-up and Extension Ideas

- Ask the children for their own opinions on the incident.
- Ask them to develop their ideas regarding traffic control. (Link this to the instruction under Now on activity sheet **Which is Which?**, page 19.) For example, the children could consider how the cows would have caused fewer problems if, for example, the area had been a shopping precinct. Link this to Geography and local studies.
- The children can share their ideas for 'Rules for walkers' (**What Comes Next?**, page 18) and write a countryside code. Discuss also the best way of presenting the code, for example, as a poster using bullet points, whether or not to include illustrations and captions and so on.
- The work on fact and opinion can be a useful introduction to the study of more complex material, such as historical sources. Those children who have a good grasp not only of the differences between fact and opinion, but also of the subtleties involved, can approach this with some confidence. For example, when studying cultures in the distant past, such as Egyptian culture, insufficient or contrary evidence may lead to different viewpoints or reserved judgements.

Cows on the Move

Study the illustration below.

Talking and Thinking

- Find each cow and say where it is.
- What problems have they caused?
- What are the people doing?
- Choose three people in the picture and discuss:
  - how they feel
  - where they think the cows have come from
  - why they think the cows are there.

What Comes Next?

Number the sentences in order to explain what happened.

- [ ] Four cows left the herd and wandered through the gate.
- [ ] They travelled up the lane towards the crossroads.
- [ ] Someone left the gate open.
- [ ] A herd of cows was grazing in the field.
- [ ] They caused several problems at the crossroads.
- [ ] They wandered on to the lane.

Write down five rules for walkers in the countryside.

Which is Which?

1. Read the comments. They are either:
   - **fact** (true)
   - **opinion** (someone's point of view).

2. Tick the correct box for each comment.

	Fact	**Opinion**
A		
B		
C		
D		
E		
F		
G		
H		

NOW Imagine you are a shopkeeper in this area.
Write three factual comments you could make.
Write three opinions you could make.

Y4 12/6/01.

ideas page

Points of View

Background

The children are asked to consider different viewpoints focused around the building of a nature park. One of the key issues is that it will replace an existing though dilapidated playground. This makes it a more difficult decision for the children to make. The activity sheets are intended to help them organise and write down their ideas. The first activity sheet asks the children to make simple notes, emphasising the need to isolate the main points (an example is given). The second sheet follows on from this, by which time the children should be clear about their points of view.

Learning Objectives

- To consider different viewpoints
- To suggest solutions
- To make notes
- To make decisions

Introduction

- The children should study the map on the resource page **Dove Lane Nature Park** first. This will allow them to see possible solutions to some of the problems presented underneath.
- Ask them to identify the comments that are in favour of the nature park and those that are against and then consider solutions. (For example, the nature park could be sited on the north side of the main park, away from the residential area and could also incorporate the pond and café.) You may wish to record the children's suggestions.
- Other potential problems might be: preference for a better playground, such as an adventure playground; objections to the original, and more formal park design being changed.
- Other reasons in favour of building the nature park might be: it involves all members of the community, not only children; city dwellers will have a greater opportunity to relate to nature.

Using the Activity Sheets

For and Against
The children will need a copy of the resource page to complete this sheet. The children might find it helpful to cut out the reasons for and against the nature park from the resource page, add their own on paper or card and then sort them into the 'For' and 'Against' columns. This sheet also offers the children an opportunity to practise their note-making skills. Underlining key words will help them note the important words.

Making Decisions
To complete this writing frame the children should be clear about whether or not they are for or against the nature park and the main reasons for their decision. They should also be able to say what considerations have been taken into account (such as finding solutions to problems or justifying their decision further).

Follow-up and Extension Ideas

- The children could use ICT to make a data bank of their findings. They could construct graphs and pie charts to show the proportions for and against the nature park.
- The work could be extended so that some children could debate whether an adventure playground or a nature park should be built. They could work in groups adding reasons for and against both propositions and then attempt a debate with you as chair.
- The children can use the methods outlined in the chapter to study a local issue. However they will need to focus on specific features, otherwise they are likely to become overwhelmed with information. For example, one group of children could look at the problems created for local residents, another the value of such a project. Furthermore, they will almost certainly need to carry out some fieldwork and use more specific geographical skills. For example, they may need to locate information on a local map, be able to study a range of sources, such as photographs and newspaper articles, and have developed some practical skills such as how to use a camera.

Dove Lane Nature Park

Dove Lane Nature Park, will have animals such as deer, goats and rabbits and a bird sanctuary. It will be built in the middle of a large city in the main park, on the site of an old playground. Some people are for the project. Others are against it.

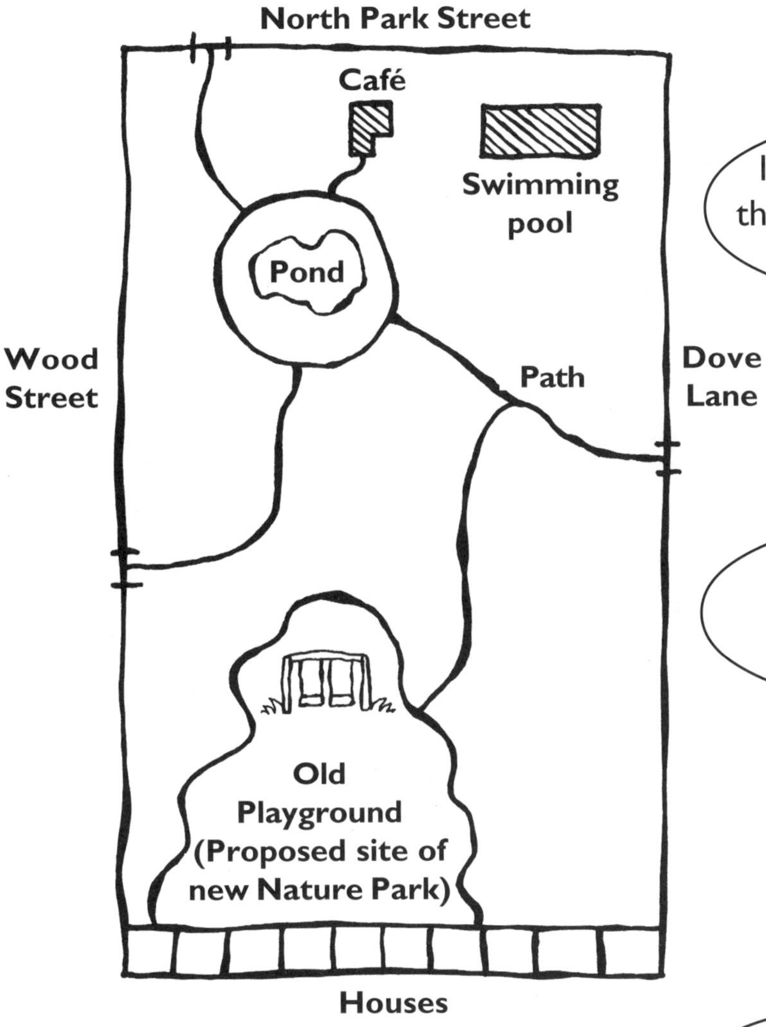

Talking and Thinking

- First study the map to see where the nature park will be and what is already in the main park.
- Then read what the people say about the project. Decide what they mean and whether they are for or against the nature park.
- Can you see how any of the problems could be overcome?
- Can you think of any more problems that could arise?
- Can you think of any more reasons for building the nature park?

For and Against

1. Make notes listing the reasons for and against the nature park. Use only a few important words. The first has been done for you.

Nature Park Project	
For	Against
Everyone can visit	

2. Write down any ways you think the problems could be overcome.

3. Write down any other problems there might be.

NOW Underline the points you think are the most important.
Use them to help you reach a final decision.

Making Decisions

There are two main reasons why I am for/against the nature park project.

One reason is ______________________________

____

____

____

The other reason is ______________________________

____

____

____

I would also like to add ______________________________

____

____

____

NOW Find out if there are plans for new buildings (or knocking down old buildings) in your local area. (For example, it might be the building of a new supermarket.) Find out where the building is planned and who will be affected by the changes.

ideas page

Newspapers

Background

The resource page **The Daily Shout** provides an example of the front page of a newspaper along with labels and contents. (The latter is often found on the second page, with a 'quick index' on the front.) It would be useful to compare this resource page with **The Pipsqueaks** (page 13) to highlight the different purposes of comics and newspapers. It is suggested that you have a range of newspapers to hand for the children to study.

The first activity sheet focuses on headlines; the second is a writing frame which asks the children to assess what they have understood.

Learning Objectives

- To be aware of the layout and features of newspapers
- To understand common terminology
- To compare the front page of a newspaper with a comic
- To understand:
  - the purpose of newspapers
  - who the audience is
  - why newspapers have advertisements

Introduction

- Begin by asking the children to consider the layout of the front page and what they think the labels refer to. You may wish to compare the distribution of photos and text of tabloid and broadsheet front pages.
- Discuss the contents again, ensuring the children understand the terms used (such as 'editorial', 'classified' and 'features').
- Ask what they think the purpose of the front page is and of newspapers in general, comparing their purpose with that of comics.
- The children should also understand that newspapers make money from advertising.

Using the Activity Sheets

Looking at Headlines

Headlines do not necessarily provide clues to the content of the article. They often use puns or play with meanings, use slang or colloquialisms and refer to topical issues that are unfamiliar to children. Although this activity sheet is concerned with matching headlines to their articles or meanings, the children can do this by using contextual clues. However, they may not be familiar with sayings such as 'pipped at the post'. The extension work therefore asks them to explain their choices to a partner and you may wish to discuss double meanings and homonyms (two or more words with the same spelling, but different meanings) with them. It is only through experience that they will come to understand such language use.

Looking at Newspapers

This activity sheet offers the children an opportunity to record what they could and could not understand in a newspaper. It is best if they focus on two pages only, each from a different newspaper, but dealing with the same issue. (For example, the sports page from a tabloid and a broadsheet, or the front page of a local newspaper and a daily.) They could approach the task from a variety of angles, such as deriving clues from photos and captions, recognising layout and content and recording unfamiliar terms or names. Discussing their findings in a group or with a partner subsequently should be helpful.

Follow-up and Extension Ideas

- Provide the children with plenty of opportunities to examine newspapers. They should be able to find their way around and understand the likely content before beginning a class newspaper.
- Most weeklies and some dailies include a range of supplements designed to increase sales. Their sheer weight and quantity can be daunting. Discuss the purpose, value and time involved in reading these.
- Studying local newspapers can be useful since they are closer to the type of newspaper the children will design. National or international issues (such as pollution, disasters, elections or transport) can still be discussed from a parochial perspective.
- Once the children are familiar with newspapers they can begin their own. Several of the chapters in this book covering fact, opinion, point of view, bias and reporting will be useful here.

The Daily Shout

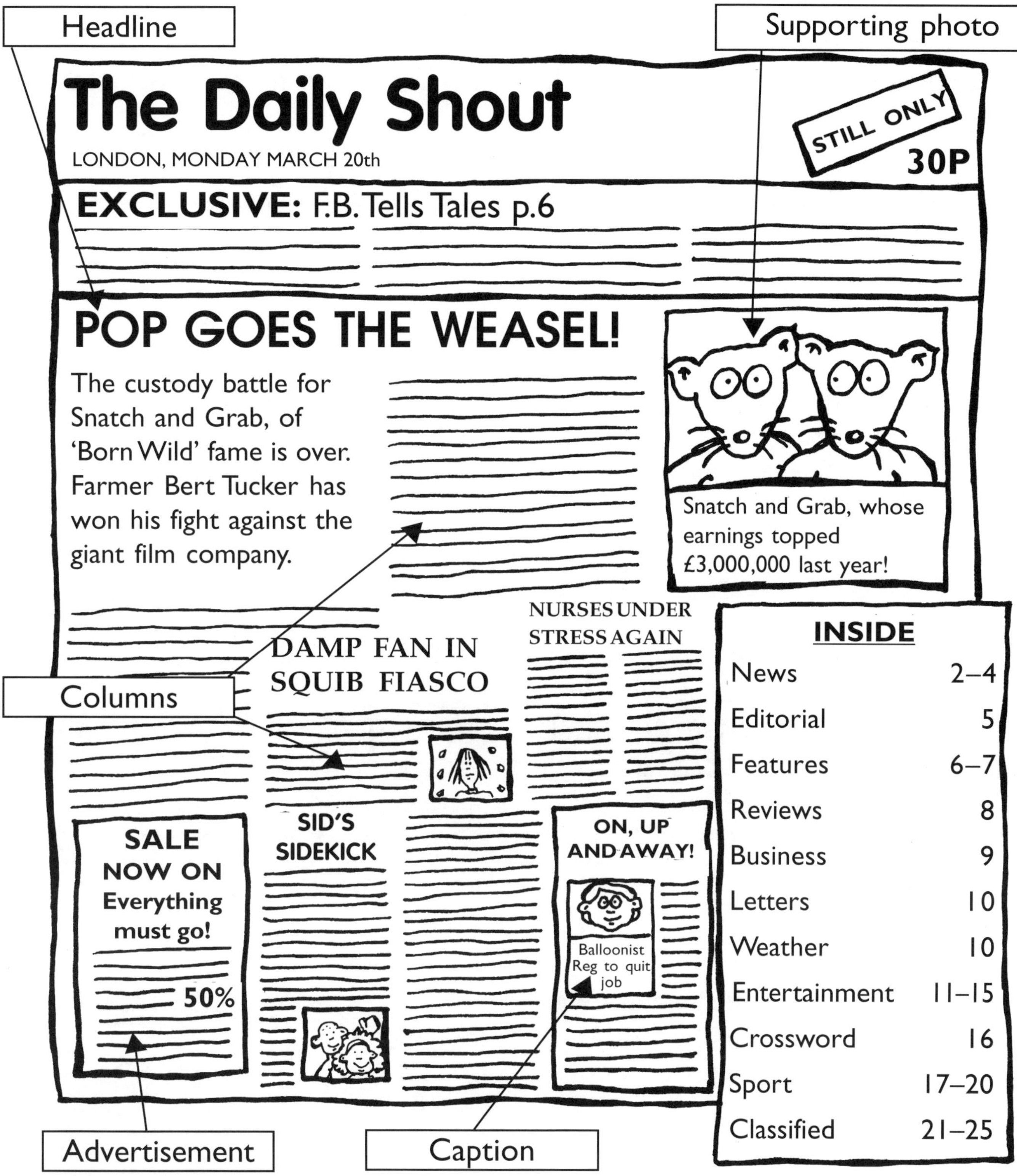

Talking and Thinking

- Study the front page and labels and explain what they mean.
- Do you have newspapers at home? If so, who reads them? Think of three reasons why each person reads the newspaper.
- Study 'Inside' and decide what the list refers to.
- What does 'exclusive' mean? What section does it come under?
- Why do you think newspapers have **advertisements**?

Looking at Headlines

Headlines are meant to attract attention, but their meaning is not always clear, until you start to read the article. Match each headline to its **article**.

Cool Cats in Kipper Crisis | A NOD AND A WINK | **Cash Stash**

From Hound to Found | STARS IN HER EYES | Pipped at the Post

a) Barney, famous for advertising dog food, has been reunited with...
b) Two children stumbled across a holdall containing £10,000 in a local...
c) Pet owners have been requested to keep their moggies indoors at night after complaints from a local fish-curing factory...
d) The Post Office has refused to deliver thirty-three boxes of rotten apples...
e) A world tiddlywinks tournament has received the go-ahead...
f) A new planet has been discovered by an unknown female astronomer...

These headlines have **two** meanings each. Try to match them.

STORM IN A TEACUP | Lucky in Love

Mouse Finds New Home | **Banks Break under Pressure**

a) A couple celebrate their sixtieth wedding anniversary.
b) Predictions of bad weather are proved wrong.
c) Lucky the dog is the constant companion of Tibby the cat.
d) A river overflows causing flooding.
e) Villagers protest over the closure of a local café.
f) The earliest hand-held device for use with a computer is given to a museum.
g) Striking bank employees win a pay rise.
h) A white mouse finds new owners after a television appeal.

NOW

- Work with a partner. Take it in turns to explain your answers to each other.
- Did you understand all the headlines?

Looking at Newspapers

I have been studying these pages from two different newspapers.

Newspapers	Pages

The easiest page to understand was ____________________

This was because ____________________

____

____

and also because ____________________

____

____

I could not understand the following ____________________

____

____

In particular I would like to know what/why ____________________

____

____

ideas page

Writing a Book Review

Background

The children are asked to write a simple review of a story they have read. The resource page **Denny's Secret** provides a model. The review is written from the point of view of a child, for children, and outlines some of the features that could be included in a review. The first activity sheet, **Whose Choice?**, asks the children to consider audience range, and the second, **Writing a Review**, provides a structure for the children to write their own review.

Learning Objectives

- To identify the features of a book review (for fiction)
- To identify who the audience will be
- To consider that different books will appeal to different people
- To make notes
- To write a book review

Introduction

- Read the review on the resource page with the children.
- Ask them to identify the labels and explain what these are referring to.
- One of the main problems children encounter when writing reviews is how to summarise the story. Knowing where to begin and end is difficult and there is a tendency to say too much. The following might be useful:
  - Discuss the limited information about the story that is given in the review.
  - Stress that the children should not give the story away by saying too much.
  - Ask them to sum up in one sentence the storyline of a book they have read.
- Encourage the children to be objective. For example, discuss why some people might not choose to read *Denny's Secret*. If some children choose to write about a book they did not enjoy, they could still consider who might enjoy the book and why.

Using the Activity Sheets

Whose Choice?
The children are given information on people's tastes and hobbies and asked to consider what kind of books might appeal to them. (This activity is designed to encourage them to be objective when writing book reviews.) Some answers are clear, others might vary. For example, E might include biography (of famous sportspeople) as well as thrillers and books about sport. Any answers the children can justify should be acceptable.

Writing a Review
Here the children are asked to make notes using bullet points about their chosen book. The headings follow the labels in **Denny's Secret** with an opportunity to write additional information. By writing notes first, the children should focus on the main points more easily. This should also curb the tendency to say too much, particularly about the story. For any children who need help making notes, page 15 in this book might be useful.

Follow-up and Extension Ideas

- Ask the children to collect book reviews of children's books from comics and newspapers and to identify the sections as described on the resource sheet. Discuss any deviations from the suggested template.
- Prompt the children to write short book reviews of chosen books in the classroom and to attach them inside the front covers for would-be readers. The reviews could also be put on disk and made available to the rest of the class.
- The children could also write reviews of non-fiction books, taking into account such aspects as clarity, use of illustrations, usefulness of contents and index pages.
- Encourage the children to construct a survey to find out the reading habits of the class. They will need to classify information under book types and could construct a graph of their findings.
- If making a class newspaper, include a review section. Film, video and computer game reviews can also be included.

Denny's Secret

Book Review

'Denny's Secret' by Minnie Jacks

Main character described

Brief comment on story

Denny is a nine-year-old boy who lives with his eccentric grandmother. He has no brothers and sisters and his best friend is Pal, his street-wise mongrel dog. Together they discover a secret that changes Denny's life and places him in danger.

Style of writing

This is an exciting story written with pace. The characters are vivid and memorable. There is plenty of humour too, particularly in the character of the grandmother.

Why you would/would not recommend it

Although it is a long story (over thirty chapters) I did not get bored and would recommend it. I felt as if I was with Denny and Pal through their adventures and could not put the book down.

Who it would appeal to

If you are between eight and eleven years old, and like adventure or animal stories, you should enjoy this book. Don't be put off by its length!

Review by Lee Ong

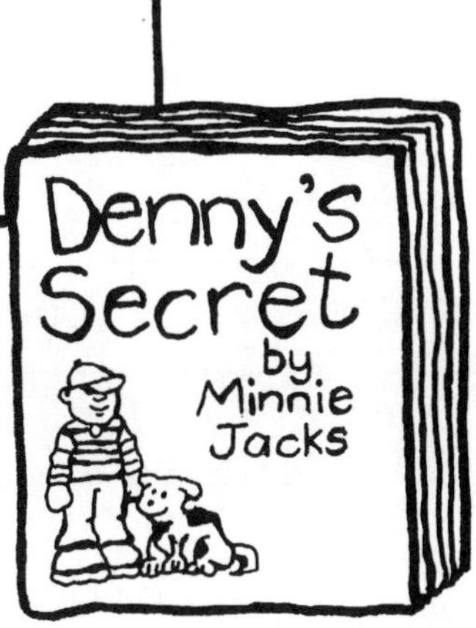

Talking and Thinking

- First read the **review** of *Denny's Secret*.
- Then read the labels. Do they describe the different sections correctly?

Whose Choice?

1. Read the information given about different people below.

A. Lennie writes his own jokes, loves poems and ghost stories.

B. Pip likes to have stories read to her. She likes to see the pictures. At home she has two hamsters, a guinea pig and a dog.

C. Bob travels on the train to work every day. He likes reading, but doesn't have much time.

D. Sunita enjoys finding out about how things work.

E. Sue is a keen sportswoman and also enjoys crime and spy stories.

F. Tom plays cricket and likes to read about famous cricketers.

2. Decide what kinds of books each person might like by ticking the correct boxes. You may need to tick more than one box for each person.

	Animal Stories	Biography	Humour	Ghost Stories	Picture Books	Poetry	Science	Short Stories	Sport	Thrillers
A										
B										
C										
D										
E										
F										

Write down the kinds of books you like and why.

Writing a Review

1. Choose a book you have read. Write down the **title** and the **author**.

Title of book ______________________________ Author ____________________

2. Now write a review. Start by making **notes** under the headings below, using **bullet points**.

Main character/characters

Brief comment on the story

Why you would or would not recommend the book

Who the book would appeal to

Style of writing

3. Think of another heading and make notes.

- Think about who will read your review.
- Then write your review.

ideas page

Persuasion

Background

The use of posters and leaflets in both World Wars was an important part of government strategy in disseminating information and misinformation and the public responded in a variety of ways. For example, gas masks during the Second World War were unpopular and people rarely carried them, particularly when gas bombs failed to materialise. On the other hand, 'Digging for Plenty' (or more commonly, 'for Victory') were successful slogans and wasting land and other resources was generally frowned upon by the public. Businesses used wartime to sell their products. One of the most successful advertising campaigns was for 'Bovril', in which humorous ways of outwitting the enemy were depicted.

Learning Objectives

- To understand historical sources
- To combine information from sources
- To understand who information posters were directed at
- To recognise different methods of persuasion
- To recognise that commercial companies can use wartime in their advertising

Introduction

- Ask the children to describe the posters A, B and C and to suggest what period they might come from.
- Focus on each source separately, asking the children to assess what the posters are persuading the public to do and what they all have in common (to repel the enemy).
- Ask the children what tactics are used to persuade. You may wish to discuss propaganda as a means of promoting the war effort.
- You may like to discuss the differences and similarities between government wartime posters and advertising. For example, both are selling ideas, but advertising is also selling a product for profit.

Using the Activity Sheets

Understanding Sources

The children will need to refer to the resource page to complete this activity sheet. They should be able to complete the table using observation and deduction, remembering that one statement may apply to more than one source. Ensure the children are clear about who Hitler was and how he is usually depicted. Answers: Source A: 1, 4, 7; Source B: 2, 4, 6, 8; C: 3, 5, 6, 8.

Methods of Persuasion

This writing frame asks the children to select one poster initially, and to write about its purpose and the methods of persuasion used. They are then asked to consider another poster in the same way. Encourage the children to make use of their newly-acquired knowledge and to see beyond the obvious. For example, when looking at 'Work hard for Victory' note that the woman is ploughing a field, ready for vegetable crops to be planted – a significant benefit for wartime Britain.

Follow-up and Extension Ideas

- The children could create their own writing frame to compare the methods of persuasion used in different posters.
- Provide advertisements from the Second World War and prompt the children to compare the adverts with the posters. Compare both types of source with modern advertisements.
- Provide the children with information related to rationing, rearing a pig or chickens in the city during wartime, persuading people to conserve and reuse materials (soap and water, for example, were limited) and ask them to design their own posters. The children can also carry out their own research using the library and ICT.

Wartime Posters

During the Second World War the government used **posters** to persuade people to help their country. It was suggested that people could protect themselves and contribute to 'the war effort' in different ways.

A.

TOPHAM PICTUREPOINT

B.

IMPERIAL WAR MUSEUM

C.

TOPHAM PICTUREPOINT

Talking and Thinking

Look carefully at the sources.

A.

- What does the poster suggest people should do?
- Why do you think they were asked to do this?

B.

- What are the man and woman saying?
- Who is under the table and what is he doing?
- Why are the words in bold important?

C.

- Who was Hitler?
- What is a gas mask?
- Why do you think people were encouraged to wear them?

Understanding Sources

You will need to use the resource page **Wartime Posters** with this activity sheet.

1. Read all the statements first.

2. Tick which source applies to each statement. Remember, a statement may apply to more than one source.

Statement	Source		
	A	B	C
1. Using land to grow food helped the war effort.			
2. The government was worried about spies.			
3. The government thought gas bombs might be dropped.			
4. This is a comic poster with a serious message.			
5. This is a serious poster with a serious message.			
6. Hitler was an enemy.			
7. There were food shortages during the war.			
8. This is a warning poster.			

Decide which poster you think the public would remember best and why. Think of at least three reasons and write down your answer.

Methods of Persuasion

I have been studying the following wartime poster: ____________________

____

It was made to persuade people to ____________________

____

____

This was because ____________________

____

It tried to persuade people by showing ____________________

____

and also by ____________________

____

Another poster, such as ______________ tried to persuade people to

____

It tried to do this by ____________________

____

____

and also by ____________________

____

ideas page

Advertising

Background

This example of an advertisement has been chosen because the children can examine it from more than one point of view: as an advert, designed to catch the eye and sell products; as a creative act or invention; as a visual joke. William Heath Robinson (1872–1944) was born in London and attended Islington Art School and the Royal Academy School. He was mainly interested in landscape painting but became a book illustrator as a means of earning a living. He moved into advertising in his thirties and during the First World War produced wartime cartoons showing a range of comic inventions. His humour, the attention to detail and the little absurdities in his work became his keynote.

Learning Objectives

- To recognise that adverts are a means of persuasion
- To recognise that adverts are designed to sell products
- To understand that humour is used to persuade
- To understand what the target audience is
- To design a product
- To create an advert

Introduction

- First discuss with the children what advertising is and its main purpose. Ask them to recall adverts they know, why they think they remember them and whether they like or dislike them. (It is also worth asking whether or not they can remember what the brand is that is being sold. Sometimes the sequence of events or story is more memorable than the product.)
- Discuss what bias and exaggeration is and why it exists in advertising.
- Introduce the resource page and ask the children to describe what the structure is for and how it is made. Note the silliness of the invention and also the careful details and the way it is made to look as though it could work.
- Ask the children to guess what the advert is for. Once they know, ask them if they think the advert would encourage people to buy ladders.

Using the Activity Sheets

The Bugmobile

Here the children are given an example of an invention and then asked to design their own. You may like to discuss with them how the Bugmobile works, referring to the written information. The suggestions given vary in difficulty – the children might like to think of their own and/or add to these suggestions. As far as possible, encourage them to design features that can be adapted to suit a variety of needs, as with the Bugmobile, and to use their knowledge of science to illustrate pulleys, electrical circuits and so on.

Just the Job

Once the children have designed their invention they are asked to explain its usefulness in order to advertise it. Several subheadings are given but they may need to be modified depending on the type of invention made. The children should also be clear about who their target audience is. The extension work involves writing the advert.

Follow-up and Extension Ideas

- Ask the children to collect a range of current adverts from newspapers to compare with **Heath Robinson Advertisement**. (They might like to consider how an advertising agency might use Heath Robinson's drawings today.)
- Ask them to collect jingles from television adverts and to decide why they are used. The children can also make a database of target audiences, by viewing television adverts over a series of days.
- The children could try to describe a common product, giving a simple factual definition from a dictionary (for example, for a car) and then write an exaggerated account of the same product, this time as a suitable description for an advert.
- Examining stereotypes in advertising is also useful. How are mothers and children depicted for example? Which adverts portray glamour, everyday life, technical know-how and why?

Heath Robinson Advertisement

Study this picture carefully. It is an **advertisement** by a famous artist called William Heath Robinson (1872–1944).

Talking and Thinking

- What is happening in the picture?
- Starting from the bottom, work out how the structure is made.
- How is it supposed to stay up? (Look carefully at the details.)
- Do you think it would work? Why or why not?
- Do you think it is meant to work? Again, say why or why not.
- Think of an easier way to rescue the cat.
- The picture is a 'comical' advert. What do you think it is an advert for?

The Bugmobile

1. Work on your own or with a partner and study 'The Bugmobile' below.

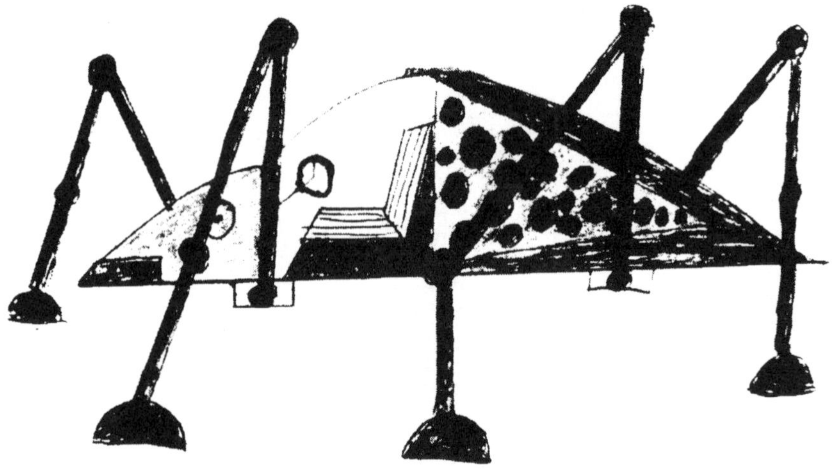

The Bugmobile

- Suckers on feet allow it to move vertically.
- It can become amphibious by fitting propellors to pads.
- Lift is devised by air pressure from feet, thrust is devised by propellor coming out of roof, enabling it to become airborne.
- Wheels fitted to legs enable it to move at high speeds for ordinary travel.
- By reversing vertically and withdrawing limbs it can move like a hovercraft.

David Karliner, aged 11

2. Design a machine or gadget using your own ideas, or choose from this list:

an umbrella that doubles as a raincoat or vice versa
a toothbrush, comb, hairbrush and mirror in one
a shoe polisher and lace-tier
a robot that will wash the car, check the tyres and change the oil
a utensil that helps you eat spaghetti
a machine that digs the garden, plants bulbs and trims the hedge at the same time

Explain, using numbers or bullet points, how your machine works.

Just the Job

1. Explain the usefulness of your machine. First write sentences by the **subheadings** below. The first has been done for you as an example. Alter it to describe your machine.

Wear and Tear *It is made of special material called 'syncrofab' which means it will never wear out.*

Time-saving

Cost

Storage

Upkeep

2. Who is your product for and why should they buy it? Write down your answer.

NOW Write an advert for your product. Refer to the work you have already done, but use bullet points and change your sentences to short comments. Include a caption to go with your drawing.

ideas page

Looking at Articles

Background

Articles on sport and the sporting world frequently have features in common, though they may vary in their complexity and organisation. Some, particularly those recounting a competition, will be chronological. Others may include biographical information on players. Others again, can be regarded as features, focusing on, for example, a team, club or player. They are all likely to use sporting terms. Many children will be familiar with these, especially football terms, but some will not and will need greater support in understanding the vocabulary. The resource page **Tough Times for Topworth** presents a short article written in the style found in a broadsheet. Typical football expressions are used but some of the words are complex. The activity sheets focus on aspects of style and content.

Learning Objectives

- To identify and understand typical features of sports reporting:
  - organisation of the report
  - terminology, expressions and colloquialisms
  - common sentence structures
  - connectives and their use
  - tenses
- To distinguish between fact and opinion

Introduction

- Read the article to the children or ask a fluent reader to do so.
- Ensure they understand the gist of the article.
- Discuss its organisation and chronology: the introduction laying out the main events; subsequent events; details of relevant past events; conclusion suggesting what is to come.
- You may also wish to compare this article to a conventional recount of a match, noting that this article is also a news report.
- Discuss difficult vocabulary and unfamiliar terms.

Using the Activity Sheets

Sports Reporting

It can be difficult for children to grasp and mimic the typical sports report style, particularly its pace and use of language. A sentence can be packed with information while another can be clipped and almost brusque. In these respects it is like much news reporting. The children are given opportunities to examine the style used and tenses are also mentioned. Note that reports are mainly written in the past tense, but not always entirely, particularly when commenting on current and future events.

Assessing Information

Here the children are asked to identify fact and opinion and to decide who the report is mainly about (Jack Payne: he is the focus in the comments by fans, by the Topworth manager, the conclusion of the article and the illustration and caption). The children might also note the implications of a long-standing quarrel between Payne and Smee.

When writing an article from a Benstead fan's point of view, the children should be aware that it is by no means clear that Smee has been wrongly accused. For example, in the past, Payne's decision against Smee has been upheld and Grimshaw has offered no comment on the incident.

Follow-up and Extension Ideas

- Discuss the issue of bias using other sports reports and articles.
- Ask the children to compare the use of language in the report with the speech in the quotations.
- Ask them to compare sports reports with other newspaper reports and draw up a list of the similarities and differences.
- Prompt the children to collect vocabulary from a range of sports and create a class dictionary of sporting terms.
- Provide the children with opportunities to read a range of sports writing, for example, stories based on sport, such as *Goalkeepers are Different* by Brian Glanville.
- If possible provide the children with opportunities to use the Internet to find up-to-date sporting information. They could write articles based on this information.
- Provide writing frames using typical sporting expressions as prompts for sentence starters, for example, 'The Open champion ...' (tennis or golf), 'The innings for...', 'Today's play...' (cricket).

Tough Times for Topworth

TOUGH TIMES FOR TOPWORTH

Six Topworth fans invaded the pitch in the second half yesterday when controversial referee Jack Payne sent off top striker Mark Smee. Accused of elbowing Benstead's midfielder, Marty Grimshaw, Smee denied the charge: "I wasn't near him – he slipped. Even Grimshaw says so. Payne has it in for me." Play was abandoned. Police and officials cleared the pitch. No other fans were involved.

Crowds congregated at the home ground this morning. "It's a slap in the face," said one fan in tears. "Payne was wrong and must go," said another. Topworth manager Bob Peel was not a happy man. Commenting he said, "This is one too far. It's one for the FA. But I don't want to say any more at this stage." Payne was not available for comment. Nor was Grimshaw.

Smee secured a header during injury time at the quarter final against Everdene last Saturday but was sent off by Payne twice last season, once for spitting during a Premiership match. Payne's decision was upheld.

Rumours suggest the FA will be called in. Close-up footage was not available.

Is the game up for Payne?

Talking and Thinking

- What does the first **paragraph** tell us?
- What happened the next morning?
- What does the last paragraph tell us?
- What do the illustration and **caption** tell us?
- Find these expressions and decide what they mean:
  Paragraph 1 – 'controversial referee', 'denied the charge', 'Play was abandoned'
  Paragraph 3 – 'secured a header', 'decision was upheld'
- Underline the following words in the **report** and decide what they mean.

invaded	accused	congregated	available	footage

- Discuss any football expressions you do not understand.

Sports Reporting

You will need to refer to the report, **Tough Times for Topworth**.

Sports reports are written in a particular style. Apart from using sporting expressions, they have other features, for example, long sentences that contain a lot of information and sentences that are shortened.

Long sentences that contain a lot of information

1. Read this sentence from the article:

Smee secured a header during injury time at the quarter final against Everdene last Saturday but was sent off by Payne twice last season, once for spitting during a Premiership match.

2. There are eleven pieces of information in this sentence! Can you find them all? Most are linked by **connecting words**, such as 'during'. Underline these first.

Sentences that are shortened

3. Read this sentence from the article:
'Payne was not available for comment.'

It really means:
'Jack Payne was not available to comment on what happened.'

4. Write long versions of these sentences:

a) Play was abandoned.
b) Payne's decision was upheld.
c) Rumours suggest the FA will be called in.
d) Close-up footage was not available.

NOW

- Study the article again. What tense is it mainly written in?
- Can you find examples of other tenses? Put a circle round them.

Assessing Information

Most newspaper **articles** contain **fact** and **opinion**. Sports reports are no exception.

1. List four facts and four opinions from **Tough Times for Topworth**.

Facts	**Opinions**

2. Do you think the article is mainly about Mark Smee or Jack Payne? Write down three reasons why. Study everything on the page.

a) ______________________________

____

____

b) ______________________________

____

____

c) ______________________________

____

____

Imagine you are a Benstead fan. Write an article for your local paper. Say what happened at the match from your point of view. Use the work you have already done to help you.

ideas page

Presenting an Argument

Background

There is an additional activity sheet included here which along with the other activity sheets and resource page can be used to help children learn how to present an argument. The resource page is part of an article from *The Guardian* (December 1996) from which the children must extract the main points. The activity sheets help them to make notes, lay out additional information about global warming and show how to pull together what they have learned. The procedure follows a logical course and largely involves cause and effect. Several pointers and organisational techniques are provided. The children can also redraft until they feel their argument is sufficiently well presented. (Each sheet can also be used separately.)

Learning Objectives

- To scan for the main points in a text
- To make notes
- To understand a process
- To combine information from different sources
- To plan a written argument

Introduction

- Read the article with the children or ask a fluent reader to read it aloud to the group. (It would be useful to have an atlas to hand to refer to the Arctic region.)
- Ask the children to summarise the article.
- Ensure they understand the terminology and vocabulary used, such as 'extinction', 'WWF', and 'tundra'.
- Turning to Talking and Thinking, discuss where and what the Arctic is and briefly what global warming is. (This is explained more fully later.)
- Discuss the main points of the article. The children can highlight these together.

Using the Activity Sheets

Making Notes

The children will need to refer to the main points of the article to make brief notes. Questions are provided as a guide – the answers needed are both implicit and explicit. Notes should be brief. Answers: A1. They are shrinking. A2. Because of global warming. B1. Polar bears need ice sheets to reach hunting grounds. B2. Ice has become too thin. B3. Polar bears starve. C1. Polar bears and seals need snow caves as shelters for young. C2. Snow caves collapse. D1. Animals will go north. D2. Because it is colder.

The Effects of Global Warming

This sheet explains global warming. The children should add additional information to show they have understood the consequence for animals of ice melting (polar bears cannot travel to their breeding and hunting grounds; shelters for the young polar bears and seals collapse). The causes of global warming are not given. Some children may be able to investigate this.

Putting an Argument Together

This flow chart sets out one possible way of combining the information the children have gathered to present an argument. (The chart could also be used to present the argument beginning with the effects of global warming on polar bears and seals and working backwards.)

Follow-up and Extension Ideas

- Discuss with the children the importance of being sure of the facts before presenting an argument. This, combined with useful cues, such as 'However...', 'In addition...', 'Consequently...' will help the children to organise their thoughts. You can also use the article on the resource page to point out the journalistic style used and the organisation of paragraphs. Those children who have acquired some skill can turn to examining arguments in which more than one case is presented.
- You may wish to discuss global warming further and other viewpoints. Although there is a consensus of opinion amongst scientists that the burning of fossil fuels is a primary cause of global warming, a few believe this may be part of a wider picture of climate change. CD-ROMs can be useful research tools here.
- You may also wish to discuss other factors in global warming such as the destruction of rainforests, which take in a great deal of carbon dioxide, and other effects of climate change, such as desertification. Newspapers frequently cover environmental issues of this sort. Again ICT can be used for further investigations.

Problems for Polar Bears

Polar bears face Arctic death as warming shrinks tundra

Paul Brown, Environment Correspondent
***The Guardian* Tuesday December 17, 1996**

Polar bears face extinction and a large number of other animals will be reduced to tiny remnant populations by global warming in Arctic regions, the World Wide Fund says in a report today.

Some of the world's last great wildernesses are under threat as the ice sheets and the tundra shrink. Polar bears need sea ice to travel to their breeding and hunting grounds. The warmer winters mean the sea ice is either too thin or has disappeared completely in some areas, leaving polar bears to starve because they cannot hunt their main prey, the ringed seal.

Even where ice remains, both the bears and seals are in trouble because both rely on snow caves within deep drifts to bring up their young. The caves form protective shelters like the eskimos use igloos, but the warmer spring means the snow caves collapse on the youngsters of both species.

Adam Markham, director of WWF's climate campaign, said in London: "The effects of warming are already being noticed. More than a dozen climate models are unanimous that climate change will continue to be particularly strong in the Arctic – especially in winter. A whole host of plants and animals could be pushed north, quite literally to the ends of the earth."

Talking and Thinking

If you can find the correct answers to these questions you will have understood the main points of the article. Underline with a red pen any words in the article that give you clues.

- Where and what is the Arctic?
- What is happening to the Arctic?
- Why is this happening?
- How does this affect the polar bear? Give one reason why.
- What are snow caves?
- Who uses them?
- What happens to the snow caves?
- Why will the animals be pushed north?

Making Notes

Read the article on the resource sheet **Problems for Polar Bears** again and make short notes under the following questions.

A. What is happening to the ice sheets and the tundra? Why?

1. ______________________________

____

____

2. ______________________________

____

____

B. How does this affect travelling polar bears?

1. ______________________________

____

2. ______________________________

____

3. ______________________________

____

C. What other problems are there for polar bears and seals?

1. ______________________________

____

____

2. ______________________________

____

____

D. Where will the animals go? Why?

1. ______________________________

____

____

2. ______________________________

____

____

NOW

- What do you think 'climate change' means?
- Write down another example of climate change.

The Effects of Global Warming

The earth is surrounded by gases that stop heat escaping, which acts rather like a greenhouse. One of these gases is carbon dioxide. When we burn fuels such as oil more carbon dioxide is produced. Carbon dioxide passes into the atmosphere, for example, from car exhausts. So gradually the earth is getting warmer. This is called 'global warming' or the 'greenhouse effect'.

1. Look at this diagram. It shows some of the effects of global warming.

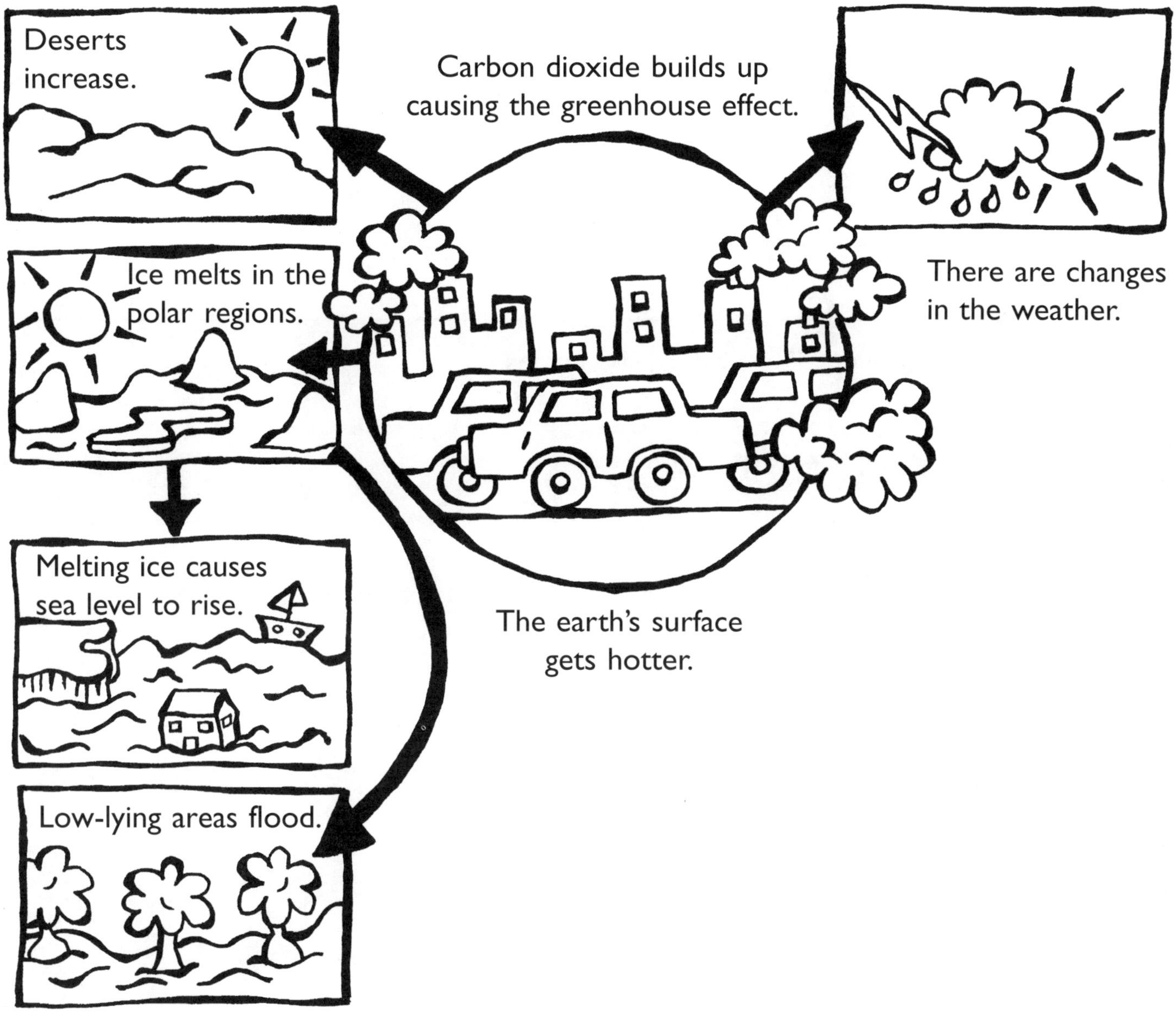

2. Work with a partner. Between you explain the effects of global warming.

3. Now add another arrow in the right place and write down how animals in the Arctic are being affected. Use the article on the resource sheet **Problems for Polar Bears**.

Putting an Argument Together

Use the ideas below to help you **present an argument** to show the relationship between global warming and what is happening to polar bears and seals. Use the work you have already done.

1. Complete this flow chart to help you link your points, then make notes in each section.

Say what the greenhouse effect is.

↓

Say how global warming affects the polar regions.

↓

Say how this affects polar bears and seals.

2. When you have completed your chart use your notes to write paragraphs for your argument, but remember, you will also need to write:
   - an **introduction** (say what you are going to write about)
   - a **conclusion** (say how we could help to slow down global warming).